Theo Smith

Learn all the key facts with CGP!

Want to remember all the key knowledge for Edexcel GCSE Business?
This CGP Knowledge Organiser is here to help!

We've boiled down every topic to the important bits, with in-depth
definitions and worked examples to cover everything you'll need.

There's also a matching Knowledge Retriever book that'll test you
on every page — perfect for making sure you know it all!

CGP — still the best! ☺

Our sole aim here at CGP is to produce the highest quality books —
carefully written, immaculately presented and dangerously close to being funny.

Then we work our socks off to get them out to you
— at the cheapest possible prices.

Contents

Topic 2.3 — Making Operational Decisions

Topic 2.4 — Making Financial Decisions

Topic 2.5 — Making Human Resource Decisions

Published by CGP.
Based on the classic CGP style created by Richard Parsons.

Editors: Sarah George, Duncan Lindsay, Rachael Rogers and George Wright.

With thanks to Victoria Skelton for the proofreading.
With thanks to Alice Dent for the copyright research.

ISBN: 978 1 83774 000 0

Printed by Elanders Ltd, Newcastle upon Tyne.
Clipart from Corel®

Text, design, layout and original illustrations © Coordination Group Publications Ltd (CGP) 2022
All rights reserved.

Enterprise

Basics of Business

BUSINESS ENTERPRISE	The process of identifying new business opportunities and taking advantage of them.
PRODUCT	A good or service provided by a business.
GOOD	A physical item, e.g. a book.
SERVICE	An action performed by other people to aid the customer, e.g. hairdressing.

Enterprise can involve starting a new business or expanding an existing one.

Purposes of Business Activity

Business activity needs a purpose, e.g.:

1 To provide a good or service.

2 To meet customer needs.

Customer needs change over time, so businesses need to change their products to keep up.

3 To add value to an existing product, e.g. by:

- making a product more convenient for customers
- building a good brand image
- improving the product's design or quality
- giving the product a USP (unique selling point) — a feature that makes it different from its competitors.

Reasons for New Business Ideas

1 Changes in technology

E.g. creating apps for new smartphones or tablets.

2 Changes in what customers want

E.g. people wanting products that are more environmentally friendly.

3 Products becoming obsolete (no longer used)

Firms may need new products to replace obsolete ones, e.g. typewriters became obsolete when personal computers became available.

New business ideas could either be original, or adaptations of existing products or ideas.

Entrepreneurs

Three Qualities of Entrepreneurs

ENTREPRENEUR — someone who takes on the risks of enterprise activity.

An entrepreneur must be able to:

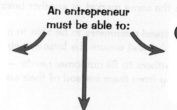

1 Organise resources — e.g. making sure the business has the right resources at the right time.

2 Take risks — e.g. investing money to start a business when success isn't guaranteed.

3 Make business decisions — e.g. deciding the business's aims, its structure, who to employ, how to grow and what to do if things go wrong.

Three Risks for Entrepreneurs

 1 Financial loss

If the business doesn't make a profit, they may lose money they invested and might struggle to pay back money they borrowed.

 2 Little job security

They might have quit their job to start the business. If the business fails, they could lose money and become unemployed.

 3 Failure

If the business fails, they might have wasted the time, money and effort they put in (that they could have used for other things).

Three Rewards for Entrepreneurs

1 Success — many entrepreneurs get great satisfaction from seeing their ideas be successful.

2 Profit — they may make more money than in their previous job if the business makes lots of profit.

3 Independence — they can choose what they do each day, and what direction the business goes in.

"It's the independence I like the most..."

Competition and Customer Needs

Competition

COMPETITOR — a business that sells the same products in the same market as another business.

Businesses need to understand customers to be able to meet customer needs — so they can increase sales and ensure the business survives.

Businesses compete with others to fill customer needs — they must persuade customers to buy from them instead of their competitors.

Five Ways to Compete

Businesses look at the strengths and weaknesses of competitors in different areas to help them decide how to stand out:

	Customer Need	How Firm Can Compete
1 Pricing	Customers generally want to pay less for products.	Reduce prices to compete with similar products (but firm will make less profit per product).
2 Customer Service	Customers want good customer service. More likely to use firm and spend more for good service.	Train staff to give good service, or provide extra services to stand out against competition.
3 Quality	Customers want good quality products.	Improve and emphasise quality of products (though this can increase costs).
4 Product Range	Customers like to have a wider range to choose from, to find a product that best suits them.	Develop new products to fill gaps in product range — there's less competition for new products and the firm appears innovative.
5 Location	Customers prefer not having to travel far or wait a long time when buying products.	Open new stores or sell online to be more convenient.

Market Research

Five Ways Market Research Helps Firms

1 Find out general information about the market, e.g.:

MARKET SHARE — the proportion of total sales in the market controlled by a business.

MARKET SIZE — how many potential buyers or sellers of products there are, OR the total value of products in a market.

2 Understand customers

Helps a firm...
- know who customers are
- know customers' needs
- know how to satisfy customers' needs.

3 Make informed decisions

Helps firms decide e.g. price of products.

4 Reduce risks

Helps firms avoid selling the wrong products (i.e. something unwanted).

5 Spot a gap in the market
(when a customer need is not being met)

Firms may fill a gap by, e.g.:
- selling in a new place
- marketing products in a new way.

Primary Market Research

PRIMARY RESEARCH — market research that involves getting information from customers or potential customers.

E.g.: observations, surveys, questionnaires, focus groups.

Businesses can use social media (e.g. Twitter, Facebook) to collect information on e.g. what's increasing in popularity.

➕
- up-to-date information
- relevant and specific to a product
- can be targeted at specific markets

➖
- needs large samples to be reliable
- often expensive
- time-consuming

Secondary Market Research

SECONDARY RESEARCH — market research that involves looking at data collected by other people.

E.g.: market reports, government reports, articles from newspapers or the internet.

➕
- cheaper than primary research
- easily found
- instantly available

➖
- often out of date
- not always relevant
- not specific to firm's product

Types of Data

QUANTITATIVE DATA — information that can be measured or reduced to a number.

QUALITATIVE DATA — information that involves people's feelings or opinions.

Reliable market research data (where results can be repeated) is important as it represents customers most accurately.

Theme 1: Topic 1.2 — Spotting a Business Opportunity

Market Segmentation and Mapping

Market Segmentation

SEGMENTATION — when people within a market are divided into different groups.

Segmenting a market can help a business aim its marketing strategy at its...

TARGET MARKET — the specific group of people that a product is aimed at.

Mapping a Market

Helps a business understand its position in the market and the market's key features.

Can make it easy to spot:
- competitors
- gaps in the market.

Three Ways to Segment a Market

1 By **DEMOGRAPHIC** — an identifiable characteristic of people within a population. For example:

Age — customers of different ages have different needs.

Income — how much people earn affects what they will buy.

2 By **location** — people who live in different areas want different products.

3 By **lifestyle** — a customer's hobbies and interests affect what they will buy.

Market maps show two variables, one on each axis. This map has a price axis and a quality axis.

Businesses or products are plotted on the map according to how customers view each one.

There are a lot of products that are lower quality and have a budget price. This is the most competitive part of the market.

Market Map for Cereal Brands

Premium Price — Meadow Made, Kickstart, Sunrise — Low Quality / High Quality — Dawn Dish, Wholegainz, Get Up!, Sweet Start, Hedgerow Bowl — Budget Price

There is a gap in the market for a higher quality product with a lower premium price.

| Use market mapping to find potential gap in market. | → | Do market research to see if demand exists. | → | If there is demand, develop new product to fill the gap and stand out from competitors. |

Theme 1: Topic 1.2 — Spotting a Business Opportunity

Aims & Objectives for New Businesses

Aims and Objectives

AIM — an overall goal that a business wants to achieve.

OBJECTIVE — a measurable step that a business uses to work towards an aim.

Five Financial Aims

 1 Survival — having enough money to stay open, e.g. to pay staff and buy stock to sell.

 2 Maximise profit — this is an aim for almost all firms.

 3 Financial security — reach a point where the business can be funded by its own revenue.

  4 Maximise sales — increasing sales helps grow market share.

 5 Increase market share — take sales from competitors or bring in new customers.

Four Non-Financial Aims

1 Challenge — some people get a sense of accomplishment from starting a business.

2 Personal satisfaction — for some, starting a business means they get to do a job that they are passionate about.

3 Independence and control — being their own boss means the owner gets control over what they do each day.

4 Social objectives — an owner can choose to run their business in ways they believe are morally right.

Factors Affecting Aims and Objectives

Size and age

 Small or new firms often focus on survival.

 Bigger firms might focus on financial security and market share.

Competition

 Firms with lots of competition often focus on survival or sales.

 Firms with little competition can focus on profits and market share.

The owner

 Small firms may prioritise personal satisfaction over e.g. market share.

 Private limited companies have shareholders, so may focus on maximising sales and profit.

Revenue, Cost, Profit and Interest

Revenue

REVENUE — income businesses make by selling products.

revenue = quantity sold × price

EXAMPLE

The stationery company Jot It Down sells 10 000 notebooks for £5 each. What is their sales revenue?

revenue = 10 000 × £5 = £50 000

Costs

FIXED COSTS — costs that don't change with output, e.g. rent, insurance, advertising.

Fixed costs are only fixed in the short term — they increase as the business grows.

Fixed costs are paid even if the business produces nothing.

VARIABLE COSTS — costs that increase as output increases, e.g. factory labour, raw materials, running machinery.

total variable cost = quantity sold × variable cost per unit

The total cost is the sum of the fixed costs and variable costs.

total cost = total fixed cost + total variable cost

Profit

PROFIT — the difference between revenue and costs over a period of time.

profit = revenue − costs

If costs are higher than revenue, the business makes a loss — the amount of profit is negative.

EXAMPLE

In May, Jot It Down has a revenue of £10 000, and has total costs of £4000. How much profit does Jot It Down make in May?

profit = £10 000 − £4000
= £6000

Interest

INTEREST — the cost of borrowing money (or the reward for saving).

$$\text{interest} = \frac{\text{total repayment} - \text{borrowed amount}}{\text{borrowed amount}} \times 100$$

This gives the interest as a percentage of the amount borrowed.

EXAMPLE

Jot It Down borrowed £5000. They paid back £5500 in total. What was the interest on the loan?

$$\text{interest} = \frac{5500 - 5000}{5000} \times 100$$
$$= \frac{500}{5000} \times 100 = 10\%$$

Theme 1: Topic 1.3 — Putting a Business Idea into Practice

Break-Even Analysis

Break-Even Points

BREAK-EVEN POINT — the level of sales or output a business needs to cover its costs.

Selling more than break-even point = profit.
Selling less than break-even point = loss.

A low break-even point means a business doesn't have to sell as much to make a profit.

Calculating Break-Even Points

The break-even point can be measured by the number of units a business needs to sell:

$$\text{break-even point in units} = \frac{\text{fixed cost}}{\text{sales price} - \text{variable cost}}$$

This is per unit.

Or by revenue needed:

$$\text{break-even point for revenue} = \text{break-even point in units} \times \text{sales price}$$

'Revenue' could be replaced with 'costs'.

EXAMPLE

Kelly's Keyrings has fixed costs of £8000. The variable cost per keyring is £3 and each keyring sells for £7.
What is the break-even point in units?

Break-even point in units
$$= \frac{8000}{7-3} = \frac{8000}{4}$$
$$= 2000 \text{ units}$$

What is the break-even point for revenue?

Break-even point for revenue
$$= 2000 \times £7$$
$$= £14\ 000$$

Margin of Safety

MARGIN OF SAFETY — the gap between current output and break-even output.

margin of safety = actual sales (or budgeted sales) − break-even sales

Budgeted sales (the sales a business expects to make) are used to forecast a future margin of safety.

EXAMPLE

Speak-eze need to sell 500 speakers to break even. Next year, they expect to sell 800 speakers. What will their margin of safety be next year?

margin of safety = 800 − 500 = 300 speakers

KEEP OUT

'margin of safety'

Theme 1: Topic 1.3 — Putting a Business Idea into Practice

Break-Even Diagrams

Features of Break-Even Diagrams

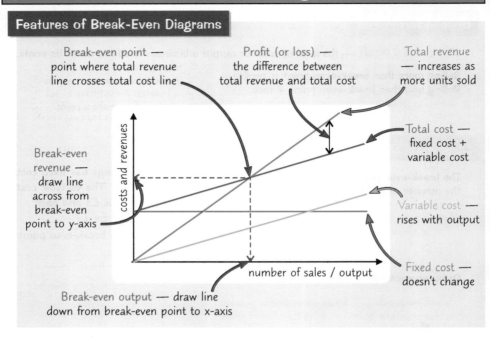

Break-even point — point where total revenue line crosses total cost line

Profit (or loss) — the difference between total revenue and total cost

Total revenue — increases as more units sold

Total cost — fixed cost + variable cost

Break-even revenue — draw line across from break-even point to y-axis

Variable cost — rises with output

Fixed cost — doesn't change

Break-even output — draw line down from break-even point to x-axis

Changing Revenues and Costs

Break-even diagrams can be used to see how changes in revenue or costs affect the break-even output.

E.g. after lowering prices:

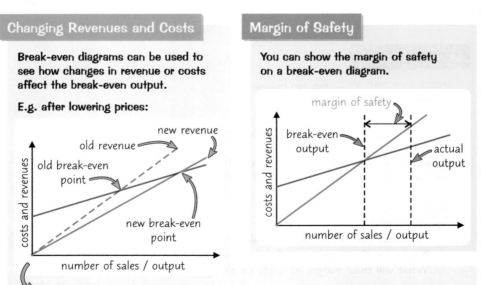

new revenue

old revenue

old break-even point

new break-even point

Revenue rises at a slower rate, so more units **have to be sold to break even.**

Margin of Safety

You can show the margin of safety on a break-even diagram.

margin of safety

break-even output

actual output

Cash and Cash Flow

Cash

CASH — money a business has available to spend immediately. Businesses need cash to pay employees, suppliers and overheads (ongoing expenses, e.g. rent and lighting).

Not having enough cash could lead to insolvency (being unable to repay debts).

A business can make a profit but still run out of cash, e.g. if they reinvest all the money they make.

Cash Flow

CASH FLOW — the flow of money into and out of a business.

net cash flow = cash inflows – cash outflows (for a given period of time)

e.g. from selling products

e.g. for wages or buying materials

Positive cash flow = more cash inflow than cash outflow.

+ no problems making payments

– losing opportunities to invest

Positive cash flow isn't the same as profit. Profitable businesses can have poor cash flow if cash inflow doesn't happen in time to meet the required outflow.

Cash Flow Forecasts

CASH FLOW FORECAST — shows the cash expected to flow into and out of the business over time. Used to show when a business won't have enough cash.

Opening balance = closing balance of previous month

Cash Flow Forecast — Sweetie Chocs			
	Dec	Jan	Feb
Total receipts (cash inflow)	7000	800	5500
Total payments (cash outflow)	4500	4500	4000
Net cash flow (inflow – outflow)	2500	(3700)	1500
Opening balance (bank balance at start of month)	1000	3500	(200)
Closing balance (bank balance at end of month)	3500	(200)	1300

Net cash flow is negative in January — outflow is greater than inflow.

Numbers in brackets are negative.

Closing balance = opening balance + net cash flow

They will need extra finance in January — knowing this in advance means they can plan ahead.

Theme 1: Topic 1.3 — Putting a Business Idea into Practice

Sources of Finance — Small Businesses

Five Reasons New or Small Businesses Need Finance

1 Start-up capital to set up the business.

2 To cover poor initial cash flow.

3 To cover a shortfall in cash, e.g. because of delayed payments from customers.

4 To cover day-to-day running costs of struggling businesses.

5 To expand the business, e.g. to pay for new premises or equipment.

Short-Term Sources of Finance

Trade credit — paying suppliers one or two months after the purchase.

➕ time to earn money to repay debt

➖ late repayment = large fees

Overdrafts — taking more money out of a bank account than is actually in it.

➕ can make payments on time without having the cash

➖ high interest rate, bank can cancel overdraft, bank can repossess assets if not paid back

> If only Kyle had repaid his overdraft, he would still have his favourite hat.

Long-Term Sources of Finance

Loans — borrowing money, e.g. from a bank.

➕ quick and easy, lower interest rate than overdrafts

➖ making monthly payments increases fixed costs, bank can repossess assets if not paid back

Personal savings — owner can invest their own money.

➕ easy, no interest payments

➖ owner could lose their money if business fails

Retained profit — the owners invest profits back into the business.

Share capital — individuals buy shares and get part ownership in the business. The business can use the money they raised from issuing shares.

Venture capital — money raised through selling shares to individuals or businesses who specialise in funding new or expanding firms. May expect returns sooner than other shareholders.

Crowd funding — lots of people contribute a small amount of money, sometimes for a reward. Often used for creative or innovative businesses and takes place online.

Theme 1: Topic 1.3 — Putting a Business Idea into Practice

Business Ownership Structures

Unlimited vs Limited Liability

UNLIMITED LIABILITY — business owners are liable for paying back all debts if the business fails (even if they have to sell everything they own).

LIMITED LIABILITY — company is liable for paying back debts, not the owners. They only risk losing the money they have invested.

Sole Traders

 Most small businesses, e.g. plumbers, hairdressers

SOLE TRADER — a business with just one owner. (They can have other employees.)

➕ Advantages

- easy to set up
- full control over business and profit

➖ Disadvantages

- responsibility can mean long hours and few holidays
- unlimited liability
- hard to raise money
  Banks see sole traders as risky.
- unincorporated

The business has no legal identity — suing the business means suing the owner.

Partnerships

 E.g. solicitors, doctors' surgeries

PARTNERSHIP — a business owned by a group of partners. Partners usually have an equal say in the business and equal shares of the profits.

➕ Advantages

more owners
= more...
- ideas
- skills
- capital (money)
- people to share work

➖ Disadvantages

- unlimited liability (usually)
- each partner is legally responsible for all the others
- partners have to share profits
- partners might disagree on business decisions

This means the business has a separate legal identity from its owners.

Private Limited Companies

PRIVATE LIMITED COMPANY — a business that is incorporated and owned by shareholders. Shares can only be sold when all shareholders agree.

Private limited companies have 'Ltd.' after their name.

➕ Advantages

- limited liability
- easier to get loans

➖ Disadvantages

- expensive to set up
- required to publish accounts every year

Franchises and Business Location

Franchising

FRANCHISE — an agreement where one business pays to sell another business's products or use its ideas/trademarks.

FRANCHISOR — the established business that allows another firm to sell its products or use its ideas/trademarks.

FRANCHISEE — the new business buying into the franchise.

Franchisees can trade under their own name (e.g. car dealerships) or use the name of the franchisor (e.g. fast-food restaurants).

 Advantages

- brand recognition can help sales
- can be easier to get loans (seen as less risky)
- franchisor might help franchisee with e.g. training, management

Disadvantages

- less freedom — limited by franchisor's rules
- extra costs from payments to franchisor

Four Factors Affecting Business Location

  Competition

Being near competitors means skilled labour and suppliers are easier to find.

Competition can mean losing sales or having to reduce prices.

LOCATION

  Labour supply

Areas with high unemployment have good labour supply and lower wages.

Towns and cities might have colleges that can provide training.

  Raw materials

Lower transport costs if raw materials are nearby.

Effects of the Internet

Business location is more flexible due to the internet:

 E-commerce means businesses can locate further from their market and closer to raw materials.

 Some businesses don't need fixed premises for shops (due to e-commerce) or offices (due to working from home).

  Market location

Cheaper to transport finished product if customers are nearby.

Businesses that rely on passing trade must be easy to get to.

Priorities depend on the nature of the business. E.g. if raw materials are hard to transport but the product isn't, it's best to be near raw materials.

The Marketing Mix

Four Elements to Marketing

  Product

The product must fulfil customers' needs or wants.

  Price

Customer must think the product is good value for money.

These four Ps make up the marketing mix.

  Promotion

Potential customers need to know the product exists and want to buy it.

  Place

Customers need to be able to buy the product — e.g. in a shop, online or straight from the producer.

> The different elements of the marketing mix affect each other. E.g. people will pay more if they think the product is high quality.

Sandra was very pleased with her new marketing mix.

Technology and Marketing

 E-commerce provides a new place for businesses to sell products.

 Digital communication provides new ways to promote products, e.g. by email or on social media.

> Firms need to adapt their marketing mix to reflect customers' changing needs. E.g. products with older technology may no longer meet the needs of customers, so have to be sold at a lower price to compete.

Competition and Marketing

Businesses might change their marketing mix to respond to competition by e.g.:

 lowering prices to make their products more attractive than competitors' products.

 developing new products to match a competitor's range or offer something unique.

 spending more on promoting their products so they seem more appealing.

Business Plans

Uses of Business Plans

BUSINESS PLAN — an outline of what a business will do and how it will do it.
Can be used to plan new businesses or to make changes to existing businesses.

Four ways business plans can be useful:

1) Forces owner to think carefully about the business's needs, and work out the cost of the idea.

2) Can prove to financial backers that the idea is worth investing in.

3) Provides an opportunity to identify and reduce risks — or to realise the business is actually a bad idea.

4) Helps people make decisions, e.g. what objectives should be set to achieve aims, how much stock to buy.

Features of Business Plans

Business idea — what the business is all about. Could include unique selling points of the product.

Business aims — usually very general, e.g. becoming the market leader in a certain area.

Business objectives — more specific than business aims, e.g. a target number of sales in a certain period.

Target market — who the business will sell to, using market research to show the target market is interested.

Forecasts — the projected cash flow, and estimates for revenue, profit and costs.

Finance — how much money is required and who will provide it.

Marketing mix — how the business will use the four Ps to sell products.

Location — where the business will locate, and why.

BUSINESS PLAN: Geraldine's Ices

Theme 1: Topic 1.4 — Making the Business Effective

Stakeholders

Influence of Stakeholders

STAKEHOLDER — anyone who's affected by a business.

Businesses are also affected by stakeholders, as their opinions must be considered when making business decisions. Different stakeholders can have conflicting opinions, so businesses need to decide who to listen to in each situation.

When selling hiking gear, it's important to keep your stickholders happy.

Seven Examples of Stakeholders

Shareholders get paid dividends when the firm makes profit.

Stakeholders	Like objectives based on...	Reason
① Owners / shareholders	Profitability and growth	They get more money.
② Managers and other employees	Profitability and growth	Better job security and career prospects.
	Ethics	Better wages and working conditions.
③ Suppliers	Profitability and growth	They get more custom.
④ Local community	Profitability and growth	May provide new jobs and mean people have more money to spend in local shops.
	Ethics and the environment	Local environment isn't harmed, e.g. by noise or pollution.
⑤ Government	Profitability, growth and job creation	More money from taxes.
⑥ Customers	Customer satisfaction	High quality products and low prices.
⑦ Pressure groups	Often ethics and the environment	They have strong views on certain subjects.

Pressure groups are organisations that try to influence what people think about a certain subject, e.g. animal welfare. They can create bad publicity if they don't agree with a business's actions.

Technology and Business

E-Commerce

E-COMMERCE — buying and selling products using the internet.

+ Convenient for consumers as they can buy from all over the world whenever suits them.

+ Good for firms as they can reach wider markets.

Firms need to adapt to the growing need to use e-commerce by e.g.:

 building websites,

 employing IT specialists,

 developing ways to distribute to online customers.

Six Methods of Digital Communication

1 Websites

 Useful for a wide range of stakeholders. E.g. can provide product information for customers and publish reports for shareholders.

2 Apps

 Used to communicate mainly with customers, e.g. about products and promotions.

3  Social media

 Good way to communicate with a large group of people at once. Often used for customer service and promotion, e.g. to advertise products or events.

4 Email

 Quick and easy way to communicate either with individuals or a larger group of people.

5 Video calls

 Convenient way to have meetings with stakeholders based in different locations, e.g. employees on different sites.

6 Live chats

 Instant messages often used for customer service and communication between employees.

Theme 1: Topic 1.5 — Understanding External Influences

More Technology and Business

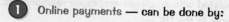
Three Examples of Payment Systems

1 Online payments — can be done by:

- Entering credit or debit card details on an app or website.
- Using an online payment system such as PayPal.

These systems mean you don't have to enter card details on every website you buy from, so there's less chance of having card details stolen.

2 Chip and PIN — customer puts their payment card into a terminal at the checkout and enters their unique PIN to pay.

3 Contactless — customer holds their payment card or smart device near the terminal to pay.

Having fast and safe ways to pay can encourage customers to buy, and means that more customers can be served in a given time.

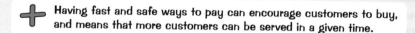
Three Impacts of New Technology on Business

1 Marketing mix — e.g. e-commerce means it's easier for firms to sell products to a wider area, which could affect how a firm prices and promotes products.

2 Costs — high costs initially but lower costs in the long term. E.g. it costs a lot to invest in new technology and train staff, but this can help people work more efficiently so fewer people are needed to carry out tasks.

3 Sales — sales increase, e.g. because apps and websites can make it easier for customers to find and purchase products.

Technology affects the products available to customers and how they are made and sold. Firms need to adapt to changes in technology so they stay competitive.

Employment Law

Law and Recruitment

EMPLOYMENT LAW — different laws associated with employer-employee relationships.
All employees must have a legal right to work in the UK —
this can mean extra work for a firm (e.g. checking documents).

Pay

There's a minimum amount that firms need to pay their workers:

- National Minimum Wage (NMW) — for workers aged 22 and under, but of school leaving age.
- National Living Wage (NLW) — for workers aged 23 and over. Slightly more than the NMW.

These amounts are usually increased every year.

Health and Safety

Effects of pay laws on businesses:

+ Potentially better motivated staff and higher productivity.

Health and safety laws mean firms need to:

- carry out risk assessments to identify possible workplace dangers,

Can increase costs, which could mean:

higher prices → reduced sales → reduced income → fewer employees

- take reasonable steps to reduce risks,
- provide staff with health and safety training and suitable safety equipment.

Effects of health and safety laws on businesses:

+ Reduces staff health problems and injuries (so less chance they'll need time off work).

Higher costs (e.g. paying for training courses).

Discrimination

Equality Act 2010 — employers can't discriminate against anyone because of e.g.:

race	sexual orientation	age
religion	disabilities	gender

Breaking Employment Laws

This affects recruitment and pay —
all employees must be paid the same for
doing the same job, or work of equal value.

Firms have a responsibility to make sure employees
don't discriminate against others either — they may
need to write policies and train staff about equal rights.

Potential impacts:

- Compensation costs
- Fines
- Bad publicity
- Closure of the firm

Theme 1: Topic 1.5 — Understanding External Influences

Consumer Law

Consumer Rights Act 2015

The Consumer Rights Act 2015 covers how products can be sold — it aims to protect the consumer.

Three criteria a product needs to meet:

1 Be fit for purpose — it has to do the job it was designed for.

Greg wondered if he should have checked the product description more closely.

2 Match its description:
- It needs to match its trade description (the way the business describes it in terms of e.g. its size, quantity, materials, properties).
- It's illegal to say that a product has been endorsed by a person or organisation unless it really has been.

Three Impacts of Breaking Consumer Law

1 Customers can ask for their money back, a repair or a replacement — this costs the business money.

2 Customers could take the business to court, which can be very costly.

3 The business could get a bad reputation, which could reduce sales.

3 Be of satisfactory quality — it should be well made and shouldn't cause problems for the buyer (e.g. a fridge shouldn't be excessively noisy).

Following Consumer Law

Firms need to:

- Train staff properly, so they don't mis-sell products and know what to do if a customer isn't happy.

- Keep up to date with changes in the law, and make changes to their business if needed, e.g. by retraining staff.

This is true for all laws that affect a business, not just consumer law.

Theme 1: Topic 1.5 — Understanding External Influences

Unemployment and Government Taxes

Downsides of Unemployment for Businesses

Different economic conditions, e.g. unemployment or inflation, change the economic climate. This can have a big effect on firms, but they can't control it

Lots of people unemployed.

→ Demand for products falls.

People have less disposable income (money left after they've paid tax).

Sales fall.

Firms respond, e.g. by reducing prices, reducing output, making staff redundant.

Firms may need to spend money retraining new workers who had been unemployed.

Potential Benefits of Unemployment for Businesses

These factors may encourage a business to grow when unemployment is high.

1 Less money spent on wages — lots of people wanting a job means people may be prepared to work for less money.

2 Easier to recruit — there are lots of people available to work.

3 Government grants — the government may give grants to firms who provide new jobs in areas of high unemployment.

Government Taxes

Tax rates are set by the government. Both consumers and businesses pay tax, e.g.:

Consumers pay income tax (tax on money they earn).

Businesses pay tax on their profits, tax on premises they own, and environmental tax on activities that harm the environment.

Changing tax rates can affect a business, e.g.:

income tax rates reduced → consumers have more disposable income → sales increase

If income tax rates increase, the opposite could happen.

business tax rates increased → business has less money to reinvest → business growth is slower

If UK business tax rates are reduced, businesses have more money to reinvest. However, more firms from abroad might relocate to the UK, increasing competition.

A business may try to avoid this by e.g. finding ways to pay less tax, cutting costs elsewhere, or relocating to a country with lower tax rates.

Inflation and Consumer Income

Inflation

INFLATION — the increase in price of goods and services over time.

The rate of inflation is calculated by tracking the prices of regular household products over time.

Possible effects of high inflation on businesses:

Short-term increase in sales — customers quickly buy products before prices go up even more.

Increase in labour costs — workers want higher pay so they can afford to pay the higher prices for things.

Sales from exports fall — products made in the UK become more expensive, so people in other countries are less likely to want to buy them.

High inflation generally means low business growth — it's hard to predict what will happen to costs and sales, so businesses are reluctant to take risks and invest in their business.

Consumer Income

Consumer income (the amount that consumers earn) increases over time.

If consumer income rises at a slower rate than inflation...

When this happens, income is said to be going down in 'real terms'.

An increased rate of inflation was having no effect for Ahmed.

Greater proportion of people's income spent on essential items, e.g. food.

Less money available for luxuries, e.g. holidays, so demand for these decreases.

Businesses that sell things at discount prices might benefit as people try to spend less.

Businesses could reduce prices or advertise more to increase demand, but this means they'd make less profit.

Businesses selling luxuries see fall in sales and profits.

The opposite is true when consumer income rises at a faster rate than inflation (i.e. demand for luxuries increases).

Interest Rates

Interest Rate Basics

% **INTEREST RATE** — a percentage that shows the cost of borrowing money or the reward given for saving money.

Lots of methods of borrowing money have interest rates, e.g. bank loans, mortgages, overdrafts and credit cards.

The higher the interest rate, the more interest you pay on money you've borrowed, and the more interest you earn from savings.

In the UK, most interest rates are linked to the base rate of interest. The Bank of England sets the base rate depending on the economic climate.

Effects of Interest Rate Changes

%⬇ **Lower interest rates** ➡ **Increased spending**

%⬆ **Higher interest rates** ➡ **Decreased spending**

If interest rate is cut...

⬇

Amount needing to be paid back on existing borrowed money may also fall.

Cheaper to borrow money. Less money made on savings.

Consumers borrow more and save less, so they have more money available to spend.

Businesses borrow more, so have more money available to invest in the business.

⬇

Demand for products goes up.

⬇

Increased investment leads to growth.

 Sales and profits increase.

The opposite is true when interest rates increase — demand for products goes down, and businesses have less money. This may lead to slower growth and cost-cutting.

Theme 1: Topic 1.5 — Understanding External Influences

Exchange Rates

Exchange Rate Basics

EXCHANGE RATE — the price at which one currency can be traded for another.

Exchange rates fluctuate — they are affected by the economy of the country that uses the currency, and by the global economy.

When importing products, a firm pays in the currency of the country the product was made in. E.g. a British firm importing goods from the US will pay in US dollars.

A Fall in the Value of the Pound

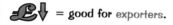 = good for exporters.

Value of the pound falls. → UK products sold abroad get cheaper. → Increased sales and profits for firms that export a lot.

Foreign products sold in the UK get more expensive. → Costs increase for UK firms importing raw materials. → May need to increase prices to cover costs. → Sales and profits may fall.

Sales may increase for UK firms that compete with foreign imports.

Fall in £ value = 'weaker' pound.
Rise in £ value = 'stronger' pound.

A Rise in the Value of the Pound

= good for importers.

Value of the pound rises. → UK products sold abroad get more expensive. → Decreased sales and profits for firms that export a lot.

Firms that export a lot may move abroad so they can trade in local currency, meaning they're less affected by exchange rates.

Foreign products sold in the UK get cheaper. → Costs decrease for UK firms importing raw materials. → Profits may rise.

Sales may decrease for UK firms that compete with foreign imports.

Theme 1: Topic 1.5 — Understanding External Influences

Business Growth

Internal Growth

 Also called 'organic growth'.

INTERNAL GROWTH — when a business grows by expanding its own activities.

➕ Advantages

- fairly inexpensive
- low risk
- slower pace makes it easier to maintain quality and train staff

➖ Disadvantages

- slow
- may require innovation (a new product or way of doing things) from within the business

Two Types of Internal Growth

1 Targeting new markets

Firm sells product to people it hasn't tried to sell to before. Can do this by:

 using new technology (e.g. e-commerce),

 setting up branches in new location (e.g. another country),

 changing the marketing mix.

2 Developing new products

Increases sales, so firm can grow. Needs innovation — often a result of research and development.

External Growth

 Also called 'inorganic growth'.

Two ways of achieving external growth:

1 MERGER — when two businesses join together to form a new, larger firm.

2 TAKEOVER — when an existing firm expands by buying more than half the shares in another firm.

➕ Advantages

- fast
- allows more control over market
- can increase market share

➖ Disadvantages

- expensive
- risky — less than half succeed
- management styles may clash
- may affect staff motivation and cause bad feeling
- uncertainty and tension from cost cutting (e.g. redundancies)

Four ways takeovers and mergers happen:

1 Join with a supplier
Allows control of supply, cost and quality of raw materials.

2 Join with a competitor
Gives bigger market share so firm is a stronger competitor.

3 Join with a customer
Greater access to customers and more control over price of products sold to consumer.

4 Join with an unrelated firm
Enter new markets and reduce risk from relying on few products.

More on Business Growth

Economies of Scale

As a firm gets bigger, costs and output increase, but output increases at a greater rate. This leads to economies of scale.

ECONOMY OF SCALE — when there is a reduction in average unit costs due to producing on a large scale.

Lower average unit costs ⟶ More profit per sale

↳ Firm can afford to lower prices ↓

Increased sales ↓

↳ Increased profits

Increase in profit due to economies of scale can fund further expansion.

Reasons for Economies of Scale

1 Buy supplies in bulk

Large firms can buy more supplies at once, which often means they can get a cheaper unit price.

2 Buy and use more advanced machinery

Larger firms can afford new technology that is often more efficient to run.

3 Bigger premises

Larger firms tend to have larger premises, which are often cheaper per unit area than smaller premises.

Diseconomies of Scale

DISECONOMY OF SCALE — an increase in average unit costs due to a business being larger.

Reasons for diseconomies of scale include:

1 Management

Bigger businesses are harder and more expensive to manage than smaller businesses.

2 Production

Production processes are usually more complex and difficult to organise for larger firms.

3 Employees

Larger firms have more people, so harder to communicate.

⟹ Takes time for decisions to reach workforce.

⟹ Employees at bottom of organisational structure can feel insignificant.

⟹ Workers can be demotivated, lowering productivity.

Sources of Finance — Large Businesses

Internal Sources

1 RETAINED PROFITS — profits that are put back into the business.

Larger businesses are under pressure to pay large dividends to shareholders, which reduces how much profit they can retain.

2 FIXED ASSETS — assets that a business keeps long-term, e.g. machinery or buildings.

Fixed assets that aren't being used can be sold to raise cash.

But there's a limit to how many assets can be sold — some are needed to keep trading.

External Sources

1 LOAN CAPITAL — money borrowed from outside a firm, e.g. a bank. It's paid back over a fixed time period with interest.

- Bank needs security for the loan — usually assets that can be sold if the firm can't pay back the loan.
- Bigger firms can get bigger loans, as they have more valuable assets.
- Established firms are seen as less risky, so they can get loans more easily than newer firms.

2 SHARE CAPITAL — money raised through selling shares in the company.

- Only an option for limited companies.
- Money raised doesn't need to be repaid.
- Selling shares reduces existing owners' share of profits and control over how the business is run.

Public Limited Companies

PUBLIC LIMITED COMPANY (PLC) — a business that is incorporated and has shares that can be bought and sold by anyone.

STOCK MARKET FLOTATION — when a business sells shares on the stock market for the first time.

Selling shares on the stock market can bring in a lot of extra finance, especially if shares are in high demand.

➕ Advantages

- more capital than non-**PLC** firms
- easy to expand and diversify
- limited liability

➖ Disadvantages

- lots of shareholders — hard for all to agree, and profit shared between more people
- possible for one person to buy enough shares to take over the company
- accounts are public, so competitors can see if business is struggling

Changes in Business Aims & Objectives

Ways Aims and Objectives Can Change

As a firm grows and evolves, its aims and objectives are likely to change. Changes are often focussed around, e.g.:

 Choosing growth or survival

business becomes stable

aims focus on survival → aims focus on growth

business starts struggling (e.g. due to economic downturn)

 Changing the size of the workforce

 An expanding business may aim to recruit more staff.

A business that's been taken over may aim to reduce number of staff to avoid many people doing the same job.

 Entering and exiting markets

A firm may enter a new market by, e.g.:

 developing a new product

 targeting a new group of people

 selling in a new location

They may aim to enter a new market because the business is growing or because existing markets are shrinking.

They may aim to exit a market if products aren't selling well.

 Changing the size of product range

If products are selling well, a firm may aim to expand the range — make similar products with different features.

If products aren't selling well, they may aim to reduce the range and focus on promoting and growing sales for their best sellers.

External Reasons for Change

 Changes in technology

New technology is often more efficient, so a firm may change their aims so they can focus on buying technology and training staff to use it.

 New legislation

New laws may affect a firm's costs or how it has to be run. Firms may need to change their aims and objectives in order to follow new rules.

 Changes in market conditions

E.g. changes to size or competitiveness of a market might mean a firm changes its aims to focus on market share.

Internal Reasons for Change

 Performance

E.g. if firm sells more than expected, they may increase future sales objectives.

 Changes in firm

E.g. new management may have different priorities, which could change aims and objectives.

Globalisation

International Business

GLOBALISATION — the process by which businesses and countries around the world become more connected.

MULTINATIONAL — a single business that operates in more than one country.

Imports

IMPORTING — buying from other countries.

➕ Gives firms a larger market to buy from. Firms may find cheaper supplies, reducing costs and increasing profits.

➖ Leads to more competition as customers can buy from foreign suppliers, so firms may need to reduce prices to stay competitive.

Exports

EXPORTING — selling products to other countries.

➕ Gives larger market for firms to sell to. Can lead to increased sales and higher profits.

Business Location

Globalisation means it's easier to locate parts of businesses overseas, e.g. stores, factories or offices. This may reduce costs if, e.g.:

 products can be made closer to raw materials, lowering transport costs

 labour is cheaper in another country, reducing staff costs

Two Ways to Compete Globally

1 E-commerce

Firms can sell to other countries online without needing stores or infrastructure there.

2 Change marketing mix for different countries

Firms may change prices in each country to stay competitive.

Firms may target products and promotion at each country's culture.

Barriers to International Trade

1 TARIFFS — taxes on goods being imported or exported.

Keeps prices of imported goods higher than ones made in the country.

2 TRADE BLOC — a group of countries that has few or no trade barriers (e.g. tariffs) between them.

Makes it harder for firms from outside the bloc to compete in the bloc.

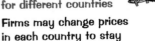

Theme 2: Topic 2.1 — Growing the Business

Ethics and the Environment

Acting Ethically

Firms can act ethically by e.g.:
- paying workers fairly and setting reasonable working hours
- paying a fair price for raw materials, e.g. using Fair Trade sources
- promoting products in an honest and fair way
- developing products safely and fairly, e.g. no toxic materials or animal testing

Ethics policies ensure firms act in ways stakeholders think is fair and honest.

✚ Advantages
- can be used to promote products
- can attract customers
- appeals to shareholders/investors
- staff more motivated and productive

⬤ Disadvantages
- expensive — firms may have to pay more for staff and materials
- may be hard to find ethical suppliers
- lower profit per product sold

There's a trade-off between acting ethically and making the most profit.

Environmental Awareness

landfill waste ← Firms harm environment by: → air pollution

noise pollution ↙ ↘ water pollution

using non-renewables

Firms can aim to be more sustainable (work in ways that won't damage the Earth for future generations) by e.g.:
- using less packaging
- disposing of waste responsibly and recycling where possible
- using more efficient machinery
- using more renewable energy resources

✚ Advantages
- appeals to customers interested in being environmentally friendly
- can give competitive advantage

⬤ Disadvantage
more sustainable processes and new equipment can be expensive — this may lead to lower profits

Pressure Groups

Pressure groups may run campaigns against firms that aren't ethical or environmentally friendly. This could damage firm's reputation and make it lose customers.

To fix this, firms can change their marketing mix by, e.g:

changing products — e.g. to use ethically sourced or environmentally friendly materials,

running promotional campaigns to counteract negative publicity.

Marketing Mix and Differentiation

The Marketing Mix

The marketing mix has four different elements: product, promotion, place and price.

Businesses can have a competitive advantage (an edge over their competitors) if they get their marketing mix right.

Differentiation

DIFFERENTIATION — making products distinctive in the market (to encourage customers to choose them over competing products).

Three ways to differentiate a product by changing the marketing mix:

  Design the product to have a USP (unique selling point).

  Promote the product in a way that makes it stand out.

  Change the price — cheaper products appeal more to mass markets, but expensive products can appeal to niche (small and specialised) markets.

Relationships in the Marketing Mix

Different elements of the marketing mix can affect each other, so firms might have to make compromises.

For example:

 Price is affected by:

Product — higher quality products cost more to make so are usually priced higher.

Place — products sold online might be cheaper as the firm has lower fixed costs (e.g. rent).

 Promotion is affected by:

Price — promotion will tend to emphasise the price if it's low, but focus on other factors (e.g. quality) if it's high.

Place — retailers with physical stores can display products, whereas e-tailers focus more on advertising.

The Design Mix

DESIGN MIX — the different elements of design needed to make a product successful.

The design mix has three main aspects:

 Function — product has to be fit for purpose, but could also have extra or unique features.

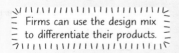
Firms can use the design mix to differentiate their products.

 Cost — well-planned design will lead to lower manufacturing costs.

 Aesthetics — product (and packaging) should look attractive and distinctive.

Product Life Cycles

Five Stages of Product Life Cycles

PRODUCT LIFE CYCLE — the different stages that a product goes through over time.

1 Research and Development (R&D) — idea is developed and turned into a product. One aim is to find the most cost-effective way to make the product.

> During R&D, big firms employ people who try to use scientific discoveries to develop new products.

2 Introduction — product goes on sale. A lot of focus on promotion to increase demand.

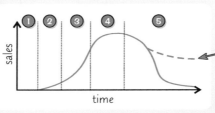

with extension strategy

3 Growth — demand for product increases and it becomes established. Firm starts to make a profit on product.

4 Maturity — demand reaches peak. Firm focuses less on promotion and more on making product widely available, until market is saturated (there's no more room to expand).

5 Decline — demand falls as, e.g. rival products take over. Firm starts making a loss on product and may stop making it.

Extension Strategies

EXTENSION STRATEGY — when a firm takes action to extend the life of a declining product. If extension strategy works, product keeps selling and makes a profit for longer.

> Firms need to find the right balance between spending money on extension strategies and developing new products.

Five examples of extension strategies:

1 Add new features — these could make product more useful or appealing.

2 Use new packaging — could make product more eye-catching so customers are more likely to choose it.

3 Target new markets — e.g. promote product to a different age group or country.

4 Change advertising — e.g. to increase awareness of the product or make it more appealing to a different market.

5 Reduce price — either permanently or by using sales promotions.

Price

Price and Demand

DEMAND (for a product) — how much of the product customers are willing and able to buy.

As the price of a product rises, demand for it tends to fall.

Firms risk not selling many products if their prices are too high.

Demand at the bookshop was at an all time high.

Internal Factors Affecting Prices

1 Technology — e.g. if a product requires expensive machinery to make, the business might have to set prices high to cover the cost. But technology can also reduce costs, e.g. by increasing efficiency.

2 Method of production — e.g. prices may be lower with flow production, as the firm is more likely to benefit from economies of scale than if it used job production.

3 Product life cycle — e.g. if the product is in the decline stage, the price may be lowered to increase demand again.

External Factors Affecting Prices

1 Competition — in competitive markets, prices can't be much higher than competitors' prices. They also can't be much lower, as people might think the products are lower quality.

2 Market segments — e.g. if a product is targeted at consumers with low incomes, it should have a low price.

3 Cost of raw materials — the higher the unit cost is, the higher the price may need to be to make a profit.

The size and age of the business also affect pricing. E.g. a larger, older firm might have loyal customers who are willing to pay slightly higher prices. However, larger firms can also benefit from economies of scale to help keep prices down.

Pricing Strategies

Price Penetration

Firm charges low price when product is new.

Helps increase demand and establish market share.

Once product is established, firm raises price to make more profit.

Price Skimming

Firm charges high price when product is new as they know the demand will be high, e.g. because the firm has loyal customers or the product uses new, sought-after technology.

High price helps increase revenue and cover cost of development.

Loss Leader Pricing

Price of product is set below the cost of making it, so firm makes a loss on each sale.

Firm assumes that selling the product will increase sales of other, profitable products.

E.g. new games consoles are often sold at a loss, but the firm makes a profit on games bought with them.

Competitive Pricing

Firm charges similar price to other firms. Usually happens if the market is very competitive and there isn't much differentiation.

Usually means little profit is made. Firm has to find ways other than price to attract customers, e.g. by providing good customer service.

A high price might also make the product more desirable to people with high incomes — this can improve the firm's image and status.

Firm lowers price once product is established to reach a wider market.

Cost-Plus Pricing

Firm decides price based on how much profit they want (while keeping demand high enough). Often happens when firm faces little price competition.

They could decide price by:

 1 Using a mark-up — adding on a certain percentage to the cost of making the product.

2 Deciding on their desired profit margin and calculating the price required for it.

Theme 2: Topic 2.2 — Making Marketing Decisions

Methods of Promotion

Branding

BRAND IMAGE — the impression customers have of a firm and its products. ◄ E.g. it's a luxury, high-quality firm.

A brand image could include a recognisable logo that customers associate with the firm or its products.

> Firms might create different brand images for different market segments. E.g. a cosmetics firm might use a different brand image for men and women.

Building a strong brand image is expensive and can take many years, but it can increase revenue in the long term, as customers are more likely to buy products made by firms they recognise and like.

Six Methods of Advertising

ADVERTISING — any message that a firm pays for to promote itself or its products.

1 Newspapers
Reach wide audience (national) or specific market (local), but poor print quality and falling reader numbers.

2 Magazines
Pricier than newspaper adverts, but better quality and targeted at specific interest groups.

3 Posters/billboards
Can be placed near a target audience and get seen often, but messages need to be short.

4 Leaflets/flyers/business cards
Cheap to produce and can be targeted at specific locations, but many people see them as junk.

5 Television
Can deliver longer message to wide audience, but very expensive.

6 Internet
Can reach wide and targeted audiences, and customers can click straight through to firm's website. But many people ignore or block them.

Sponsorship

SPONSORSHIP — when a firm gives money to an organisation or event in return for their name being displayed. ◄ E.g. sports teams and competitions are often sponsored by firms.

+ • can help raise firm's profile
  • can help target specific market segments (e.g. people who have a certain hobby)

− brand image can suffer if thing being sponsored gets bad publicity

World's Hottest Chilli Eating Championship — sponsored by Dan's Dairy Farm.

Methods of Promotion and Place

Sales Promotions

SALES PROMOTIONS — short-term methods to boost sales.

Two examples of sales promotions:

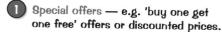 **Special offers** — e.g. 'buy one get one free' offers or discounted prices.

 Product trials — customers get free samples, often of new products.

➕ **Advantages**
- encourage new customers to try product
- boost sales in short term
- can boost sales in long term if new customers become loyal

➖ **Disadvantages**
- customers might not want to buy product when it's at full price
- might not be suitable for certain market segments (it makes the product seem less of a luxury)

New Technology and Promotion

Email — firms can send offers and e-newsletters to customers on their mailing list.

 Social media — firms' social media accounts can be used to promote products and improve brand image.

They might try to produce advertising that goes viral (gets shared and seen by lots of people in a short time period).

 Internet history — websites can track an individual's search history and location. Specific online adverts can then be targeted at the individual for products they're likely to be interested in.

Place

To make sure products are available in the right place, firms need to pick the best method of distribution.

They need to consider:
- where customers are likely to shop
- how many customers they want to reach
- how much customer service is needed
- how quickly they want to get products to customers

Two methods of distribution:

 Retailers (e.g. shops) — likely to have employees present to provide instant customer service.

 E-tailers (firms using e-commerce) — can sell to a global market and have lower fixed costs, so may be able to charge less.

Methods of Production

Job Production

JOB PRODUCTION — a method of production where each product has a unique design based on the customer's specification.

Used to make e.g. ships or made-to-measure clothes.

Advantage

Unique, high-quality products — customers are willing to pay a high price, which can lead to higher profits.

Disadvantages

• High labour costs — often requires skilled, highly-paid workers.

• Less gain from economies of scale — e.g. unlikely to buy materials in bulk.

• Low productivity.

Productivity means how many products are made in a certain time or for a certain amount of money.

Flow Production

FLOW PRODUCTION — a method of production where all products are identical and are made as quickly as possible.

Used to make e.g. chocolate bars or TVs.

Flow production is used for mass-market products — it can also be called 'mass production'.

The most efficient production is continuous — many flow production factories make products 24/7 on an assembly line. Robots do most of the work. Where people are used, they often work shifts and do low-paid tasks.

Advantages

• Gain from economies of scale — low unit costs means low, competitive prices.

• High productivity.

Disadvantages

• Capital-intensive — lots of money is needed initially, e.g. to buy machinery.

• Lots of space usually needed, e.g. to store products.

More on Methods of Production

Batch Production

BATCH PRODUCTION — a method of production where a batch of identical products is made using flow production, then materials and tools are reorganised and a batch of something else is made.

Used to make e.g. furniture or baked goods.

Batch production is a mixture of job and flow production.

Compared to job production:

- Higher productivity.
- More gain from economies of scale — e.g. can buy materials in bulk.

Compared to flow production:

- Lower productivity.
- Higher costs — e.g. more machinery and tools needed to make different products.

Impacts of Technology on Production

Advances in technology can affect how products are made, e.g. robots working on assembly lines.

New technology can also affect how products are designed, e.g. using computer software to design products, 3D printers making prototypes.

There are pros and cons of using new technology over humans:

Toy-tron 3000 wasn't sure how it ended up on the disassembly line.

 Advantages

- Increased productivity — fast and accurate work.
- Quality is consistent.
- Continuous production easier.
- Cheaper in long-term.

Disadvantages

- Expensive in short-term — e.g. buying machinery and training staff to use it.
- Inflexible — may need new technology if production method or product changes.
- Staff productivity may fall — e.g. if they're worried about losing their jobs.

Managing Stock

Just-in-Time Stock Control

JUST-IN-TIME (JIT) — where products are made just in time for delivery to customers, so stock levels are kept at a bare minimum.

Computer systems can calculate stock levels and automatically order more supplies when needed.

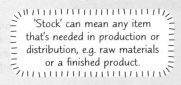
'Stock' can mean any item that's needed in production or distribution, e.g. raw materials or a finished product.

 Advantages

- Less money spent storing stock, e.g. on warehouse space and staff.
- Less chance stock will go out of date.
- Helps cash flow — minimises time between buying supplies and selling product.

Disadvantages

- Requires lots of coordination between firm and suppliers.
- Less gain from economies of scale because stock isn't bought in bulk.

Bar Gate Stock Graphs

Some firms use a production and distribution system where they have buffer stocks.

This means they're prepared if there's a supply shortage or demand rises unexpectedly.
Bar gate stock graphs are used to monitor stock levels and see when to order more.

EXAMPLE

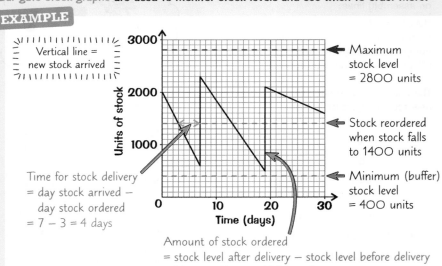

Vertical line = new stock arrived

Units of stock

Time (days)

← Maximum stock level = 2800 units

← Stock reordered when stock falls to 1400 units

← Minimum (buffer) stock level = 400 units

Time for stock delivery
= day stock arrived − day stock ordered
= 7 − 3 = 4 days

Amount of stock ordered
= stock level after delivery − stock level before delivery
= 2100 − 500 = 1600 units

Working With Suppliers

Procurement and Logistics

PROCUREMENT — finding and buying things that a firm needs from suppliers outside of the firm.

LOGISTICS — getting goods or services from one part of the supply chain to another.

Two benefits of effective procurement and logistics systems:

 Reduced costs

The business gets the right supplies at the right time (so time and money aren't wasted) and for the best price. This reduces unit costs, so the firm can make more profit on each item, or reduce prices.

 Better reputation and customer satisfaction

The business becomes known for having high-quality, reasonably priced products that are delivered on time.

Five Things to Consider When Choosing a Supplier

 Quality

Quality needs to be consistent. Customers will shop elsewhere if they're not happy with the quality of the products sold.

 Cost

Cheaper suppliers might have lower quality products.

It might be better to pay more to get e.g. better quality products or faster delivery.

 Delivery

Delivery may be cheaper and faster from a supplier that's nearby.

Delivery should be reliable — goods should arrive on time and undamaged.

 Availability

Production could be affected if a firm can't get enough supplies when it needs them.

Trust

The firm needs to trust it'll get the supplies it needs on time, and of the right quality.

Theme 2: Topic 2.3 — Making Operational Decisions

Quality and The Sales Process

Two Reasons for Monitoring Quality

1 To control costs

- Less waste from products that can't be sold.
- Less money spent compensating customers who return items.
- Less money spent on customer service as there are fewer complaints.

2 To create a competitive advantage

Being known for producing high-quality products can improve brand image. Customers may choose to buy from the firm over competitors, so they can charge more and make more profit.

Quality Control

QUALITY CONTROL — checking quality to find faults before products reach the customer.

Firms usually check:

1 Raw materials from suppliers. → **2** Random samples of work in progress. → **3** Random samples of finished products.

Firms that provide services carry out quality control too, e.g. 'secret shoppers' pretend to be customers to check the service. Poor quality service may mean staff need extra training.

The quality control process can be expensive, but still less costly than customers returning items or not buying from the firm again.

Quality Assurance

QUALITY ASSURANCE — checking quality during every stage of making a product, e.g. workers on an assembly line check their work before it gets passed on.

It aims to stop errors being made rather than having to get rid of faulty goods once they've been made.

A firm can get its quality assessed by an external body and display its rating to customers.

Six Stages of the Sales Process

1 Finding new customers

2 Approaching the customer

3 Assessing their needs

4 Presenting products to them

5 Closing (customer agrees to buy)

6 Follow-up

Customer Service

Five Ways of Providing Good Customer Service

 Have excellent product knowledge
- Questions are answered quickly and accurately.
- Customer gets product most suited to their needs.
- Customer feels confident buying from the firm.

 Have quick and efficient service
E.g. minimise number of steps needed for customer to buy a product or have an issue resolved.

 Engage well with customers
- Staff should be polite, listen to customer needs and create a positive atmosphere.
- Makes customer feel important and valued.

 Offer post-sales service
E.g. offer training to customer on how to use product, have after-sales staff available to provide support.

 Respond positively to customer feedback
- Staff should be polite, even if they disagree with customer.
- Response should be focussed on customer's feedback (not a generic response).
- Taking feedback on-board can help firm to improve customer service.

Importance of Good Customer Service

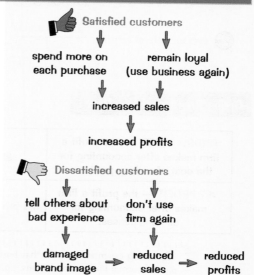

For many firms, providing good customer service increases profitability, so the benefit outweighs the cost.

Business Calculations

Average Rate of Return

RETURN ON INVESTMENT — how much a business makes or loses as a proportion of the original money put in.

AVERAGE RATE OF RETURN (ARR) — the average return on an investment each year over its lifespan.

A higher ARR is better, but what counts as a 'good' ARR depends on the type of business and size of the investment.

Two steps to calculate ARR:

1 Work out the average annual profit.

$$\text{average annual profit} = \frac{\text{total profit}}{\text{number of years}}$$

2 Use the formula to find ARR.

$$\text{ARR (\%)} = \frac{\text{average annual profit}}{\text{cost of investment}} \times 100$$

EXAMPLE

The table below shows the profit made by a business on a £2m investment over three years. Calculate the average rate of return for the investment.

	Profit (£)
Year 1	70 000
Year 2	95 000
Year 3	105 000

1 $\text{average annual profit} = \frac{\text{total profit}}{\text{number of years}} = \frac{70\ 000 + 95\ 000 + 105\ 000}{3}$

$= 270\ 000 \div 3 = £90\ 000$

2 $\text{average rate of return} = \frac{\text{average annual profit}}{\text{cost of investment}} \times 100 = \frac{90\ 000}{2\ 000\ 000} \times 100$

$= 0.045 \times 100 = 4.5\%$

Gross Profit and Net Profit

GROSS PROFIT — the profit a firm makes after accounting for the cost of making products.	gross profit = revenue – cost of sales
NET PROFIT — the profit a firm makes after accounting for all its expenses.	net profit = gross profit – ($\binom{\text{operating}}{\text{expenses}}$ + interest)

Operating expenses are costs that businesses have to pay as part of normal business operations, e.g. salaries, bills and rent.

Profitability Ratios

Gross Profit Margin

GROSS PROFIT MARGIN — the proportion of every pound spent by customers that doesn't go directly towards making a product.

$$\text{gross profit margin} = \frac{\text{gross profit}}{\text{sales revenue}} \times 100$$

Can be improved by:

 increasing price

 reducing cost of making product

Higher gross profit margin is better, but what counts as a 'good' profit margin depends on the type of business.

> E.g. supermarkets have low gross profit margins because they keep prices low to compete, but can still make large profits as they sell in high volumes.

Net Profit Margin

NET PROFIT MARGIN — the proportion of every pound spent by customers that the business gets to keep.

$$\text{net profit margin} = \frac{\text{net profit}}{\text{sales revenue}} \times 100$$

Like for gross profit margin, higher net profit margin is better, but what counts as a 'good' margin depends on the business.

> Net profit margin can decrease as a firm grows and has more costs (e.g. more salaries, more spent on rent or utilities).

EXAMPLE

In one year, Polly's Paper made a gross profit of £72 000 from a revenue of £180 000. Calculate the gross profit margin.

gross profit margin

$$= \frac{\text{gross profit}}{\text{sales revenue}} \times 100$$

$$= \frac{72\,000}{180\,000} \times 100$$

$$= 0.4 \times 100 = 40\%$$

This means for every £1 spent by customers, 60p was used to make the product, leaving 40p.

In the same year, Polly's Paper had operating expenses of £42 000 and paid £3000 of interest on loans. Calculate the net profit margin.

First work out the net profit.

net profit = gross profit —
(operating expenses + interest)

$$= 72\,000 - (42\,000 + 3000)$$

$$= 72\,000 - 45\,000 = £27\,000$$

$$\text{net profit margin} = \frac{\text{net profit}}{\text{sales revenue}} \times 100$$

$$= \frac{27\,000}{180\,000} \times 100$$

$$= 0.15 \times 100 = 15\%$$

This means for every £1 spent by customers, 15p is kept by the business as net profit.

Business Data and Performance

Using Business Data

Businesses use different types of data to help:
- track how well they're doing (their performance)
- inform about the effects of business decisions
  — data is used to support and justify making
  good decisions and to avoid making mistakes.

"This chart proves the 'free rabbit with every hat' promotion is a great idea."

Marketing Data

Firms use market research to find out how customer preferences are changing.

↓

Helps show if a decision is likely to lead to increased sales.

Types of Market Data

E.g. businesses are interested in their competitors':

market share   prices   costs of supplies

Help show if a business should e.g. lower its prices or reduce cost of its supplies.

Types of Financial Data

cash flow forecasts ⟹ help show if a decision will cause cash flow problems

(predicted) average rate of return ⟹ helps business decide if an investment is worthwhile

calculations of profit and loss, profitability ratios ⟹ help show if business should reduce costs/increase revenue

Three Limitations of Financial Data

1. Some financial data is only useful when compared to other data. It might not be possible to find useful comparisons — e.g. if one firm is much bigger than another.

2. Can be difficult to work out what caused a change, as lots of different variables affect a firm's performance.

3. Doesn't include qualitative data (e.g. customers' opinions).

Internal Organisational Structures

Four Roles in an Organisational Structure

	Role	Responsibility	
1	Directors	Decide on business's strategy with other directors at regular board meetings.	Top layer of structure
2	Senior Managers	Organise workforce to carry out directors' strategy. May be middle and junior managers below senior in larger firms.	
3	Supervisors or Team Leaders	Look after specific projects or small teams of operational or support staff.	
4	Operational and Support Staff	Given specific tasks to perform by managers, supervisors or team leaders. Not responsible for any other workers.	Bottom layer of structure

The number of people on each layer generally increases as you go down the organisational structure.

Hierarchical and Flat Structures

CHAIN OF COMMAND — the layers of management that instructions travel through from the top to bottom of the firm.

SPAN OF CONTROL — the number of workers that report to one manager.

Structure	Chain of Command	Span of Control
Hierarchical	Long — Communication can be slow and difficult as messages pass through many people.	Narrow ✚ Staff can be monitored closely, which can make firm more effective.
Flat	Short ✚ Communication can be fast and easy as messages pass through few people.	Wide — Staff can be difficult to manage effectively.

More on Organisational Structures

Centralised Structures

All major decisions are made by a few senior managers (or just one person) at top of the structure. These senior managers are very powerful.

 Advantages

- Senior managers are usually very experienced.
- Senior managers have overview of whole firm.
- Policies are uniform throughout firm.

Disadvantages

- Decisions can only be made by specific people, so decision-making can be slow — means firm can be slow to react to change.
- Depending on senior managers may cause issues if they lack specialist knowledge or make poor decisions.

Decentralised Structures

Authority to make most decisions is shared out. E.g. power may be delegated to regional managers or employees at individual branches of firm.

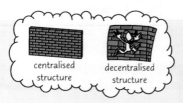

centralised structure   decentralised structure

 Advantages

- Employees use their specialist knowledge to make decisions.
- May not need central office where decisions are made, which reduces fixed costs.
- Can make changes quickly as many decisions don't need approval.

Disadvantages

- Different parts of firm may be inconsistent.
- Decision-makers may not be able to see overall needs of firm.

Changing Structures

Businesses need to choose the most appropriate structure — this may change over time. E.g.:

Small firms often start out flat and centralised.

GROWTH

Become more hierarchical — more managers are needed and business is easier to run if split into different parts.

Become more decentralised — firm gets too big for all decisions to be made at the top. Firm runs better if areas managed separately.

Communication

Effective Communication

➕ Advantages

- all staff know what they're doing and why
- staff are motivated — know what's happening in firm
- staff are confident they're doing their job properly
- different areas of firm work well together

To communicate effectively, messages need to reach who they're meant for without:

- unnecessary delays,
- being misinterpreted.

Four Barriers to Communication

1. Noise — hard to hold conversations in noisy places (e.g. factories).

2. Jargon — technical language from one department might not be understood by others.

3. Personalities — communication is difficult between people that don't get on, or that seem unapproachable.

4. Distance — can be difficult to speak face-to-face across different sites.

> Face-to-face communication is effective as body language helps express messages and it's easy to check messages are understood.

Excessive Communication

1. Inefficient

Takes time to pass on and receive messages.

Getting irrelevant messages wastes time, and may make staff pay less attention to future messages.

2. Confusion

If many people try to pass on the same message, staff could get conflicting information. Wastes time finding out what's correct and risks mistakes being made.

3. Demotivates staff

Staff can feel overwhelmed with information and annoyed if it keeps interrupting their work.

Insufficient Communication

1. Inefficient

Staff are slow to learn what they should be doing and may waste time and money doing things incorrectly.

If there's not enough communication between departments or teams, tasks may be done more than once or in ways that aren't best for firm as a whole.

2. Demotivates staff

Staff feel frustrated if poor communication stops them doing their jobs properly.

May also feel like they're not valued if not being informed about the firm.

Ways of Working

Employment by Work Time

CONTRACT OF EMPLOYMENT — a legal agreement between an employee and employer that includes details about the way the employee works.

Employment Type	Advantages for Firms
Full-time Usually 35-40 hours a week	• Employees earn more than working part-time, which can motivate them. • Staff not likely to have another job, so all work time is dedicated to firm.
Part-time Usually about 10-30 hours a week	• Useful for firms that are only busy at certain times. • Staff may be able to work different patterns, meaning they can fill in when other staff are absent.
Zero-hours Employer doesn't have to offer any work. Employee doesn't have to accept work offered.	• Useful for firms where demand fluctuates a lot. • Cheap for firms as they aren't paying for staff when they're not needed.

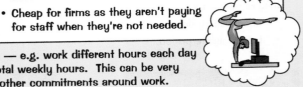

Some employees work flexibly — e.g. work different hours each day as long as they do the right total weekly hours. This can be very motivating as it's easier to fit other commitments around work.

Permanent Contracts

Employment only ends if employee:
- chooses to leave,
- is dismissed for misconduct,
- is made redundant.

Temporary and Freelance Contracts

Temporary contracts

Worker is employed for fixed time period. At the end, contract may be renewed or worker can leave.

Freelance contracts

Employees are self-employed. They're recruited for specific projects and can be hired and dismissed at short notice.

Advantages for firms:
- Easier to employ specialists without committing to employ them permanently.
- Easy to adjust staff numbers according to business's needs.

Effects of Technology on Working

Using technology has become a big part of people's jobs and has changed how they work:

- Processes are more efficient, so firms may need fewer staff.

- Intranet, video calls, mobile devices, etc. mean staff can share information and communicate more easily. It also lets staff work remotely — e.g. from home, or different office locations.

Recruitment

Two Documents for Job Adverts

1 JOB DESCRIPTION — a written description of what a job involves. Includes:
- job title
- purpose of job
- duties of job
- who employee will report to
- who employee is responsible for

2 PERSON SPECIFICATION — a list of qualifications, experience, skills and attitudes needed for a job.

Before advertising, firms need to do a job analysis, where they think about every detail of the job on offer.

Internal Recruitment

INTERNAL RECRUITMENT — existing employees are recruited into new roles within a business.
Job is advertised within the business.

 Advantages
- cheaper than external recruitment
- posts filled quickly
- candidates already know firm well
- managers already know candidates

Disadvantages
- fewer new ideas and perspectives
- need people to fill successful candidates' previous roles

External Recruitment

EXTERNAL RECRUITMENT — people from outside the business are recruited.
Job is advertised widely, e.g. in job centres, trade journals and on websites.

 Advantages
- advert reaches more people, so more likely to find someone really suited to the job
- useful if firms need to recruit lots of people at once

Disadvantages
- expensive
- candidates less familiar with how firm works

Applying for a Job

Before interviewing anyone, firms usually ask candidates for a...

CURRICULUM VITAE (CV) — a summary of a person's personal details, skills, qualifications and interests. Usually written in a standard format to state basic facts.

Many firms ask candidates to fill in an application form. These make sure firms get only the information they need, and can make it quick and easy to compare candidates.

CV — cheese violence

Theme 2: Topic 2.5 — Making Human Resource Decisions

Training and Development

Three Benefits of Training and Development

1 Staff are more productive — better at their jobs and work faster. This can reduce unit costs.

2 Staff keep up-to-date with changes in firm, e.g. they learn how to use new technology.

3 Staff are more motivated — happy knowing firm is interested in their career and progression.

This helps staff retention — more employees will stay at firm instead of moving to new jobs.

Types of Training

Staff are trained when they start at a firm, but they can also have ongoing training, e.g. to learn new processes or develop existing skills.

Two main types of training:

1 Informal Training
- No strict plan.
- Training given by other workers.
- Often done 'on-the-job' — employee shown how to do job, then improves by practicing.

+ cost effective — employee works and learns at the same time

— bad working practices can be passed on

2 Formal Training
- Set plan with learning objectives and schedule.
- Done by firm's training department or external sources, e.g. a local college.

+ higher quality than informal training

— more expensive than informal training

Staff may be encouraged to self-learn — they choose how to develop and direct their career by seeking out ways to progress, e.g. by taking online courses.

Performance Reviews

Worker and manager agree performance targets. → Training and resources are provided to help worker meet targets. → After an agreed time, worker and manager meet again to discuss how well targets were met.

Then the process starts again...

If worker meets targets, they may be rewarded with higher pay or promotion.

If worker fails to meet targets, they may be given extra training or support to improve.

Motivation and Non-Financial Methods

Three Reasons for Motivating Staff

1 Increases productivity
Workers feel valued and want the firm to do well so they do their jobs as well as they can — they complete tasks more quickly and using fewer resources.

2 Greater staff retention
Happier staff are more likely to stay at the firm, which reduces recruitment and training costs.

3 More attractive to new employees
More people will want to work for the firm, which will make recruiting easier.

Job Rotation

JOB ROTATION — a worker is occasionally moved from one job to another so they have different tasks and responsibilities.

Used when work is very repetitive, e.g. working on an assembly line.

Methods of motivating staff can be:
Financial — generally the more money a worker gets, the more motivated they are.
Non-financial — worker is motivated by enjoyment of their job and work-life.
Job rotation, job enrichment and autonomy are all non-financial methods.

 Motivates staff as they're less likely to get bored and they learn skills for different jobs.

— Jobs need to be different enough — it's not motivating if one boring job is replaced with another boring job.

This can also be good for a firm, as it's easier to switch staff round to cover absences.

Job Enrichment

JOB ENRICHMENT — a worker is given greater responsibility in their job, e.g. supervising or training new staff.

 Motivates staff to work harder by giving them new challenges.

— Staff may expect a pay rise due to their increased responsibilities. If the firm can't afford to pay more, the method may be demotivating.

Autonomy

AUTONOMY — a worker is given the freedom to make their own decisions in their job.

Workers may be told their overall goal, but not specific instructions on how to achieve it.

 Motivates staff as extra responsibility makes them feel trusted and valued.

Financial Methods of Motivation

Two Types of Remuneration

REMUNERATION — payment to an employee for the work they have done for a firm.

 Wages
- Amount paid is based on the amount of work done.
- Usually paid weekly or monthly.
- Usually how manual workers are paid.

➕ Can motivate staff to want to work more hours, as they'll get more money.

 Salary
- A fixed amount for each year, paid in instalments every month — doesn't change based on hours worked.
- Usually paid to staff who do not directly make or sell a product, e.g. office staff.

➕ Firm and workers know exactly how much they'll get paid.

Promotion

PROMOTION — when an employee is given a higher position in a firm.

- Staff can be promoted when they have gained new skills and taken on greater responsibility.
- Promotion usually means higher pay.

Even just knowing there's opportunity to be promoted can motivate staff.

Three Motivating Financial Extras

 COMMISSION — money paid to sales staff for every item they sell on top of a low basic salary.

"I'm about to lose my fringe benefits..."

 BONUS — a lump sum added to an employee's pay, usually once a year.

Usually paid to employees who have met performance targets.

 FRINGE BENEFIT — any reward for a worker that is not part of their regular income.

E.g. free gym membership, company car or staff discount.

Theme 2: Topic 2.5 — Making Human Resource Decisions